AF496537

COOKING FOR DRUNKS

Publication history

The author's moral
rights have been
asserted.

ISBN: 978-0-9957214-1-8

Art Director:
Andrew Warwick

Illustrator:
Timm Joy

Copy-editor:
Robin Black

Proofreader:
Pete Gentry

Disclaimer

COOKING FOR DRUNKS

by Andy Sausage

In Memory of Ian

CHILLY WILLY 2

KUNG POO CHICKEN 3

THAI LADYBOY SURPRISE 4

PAELLA VALENCIA 5

JAMAICAN JERK 6

SEAMAN'S FISHY PIE 7

CARNAGE CASSEROLE 8

WELSH BEANIE RAREBIT 9

TUNA PASTA CRISPY BAKE 10

PARISIAN BOLOGNESE 11

REVENGE PRAWN 12

FAB KEBAB 13

LAMB ROGAN GOSH! 14

FAJITAS 15

VERY STICKY PORK FILLET 16

MAURITIAN CRAB BOUILLON 17

GREEK ISLAND MOUSSAKA 18

MOROCCAN LAMB TAGINE 19

VENISON VINDALOO 20

MY LITTLE MEATY BALLS 21

GARY'S TEXAS BBQ BEANS 22

SHEPHERD'S PYE 23

SARDINIAN SAUSAGE GNOCCHETTI 24

PIZZA AMERICANA 25

CHICKEN PAD THAI EN CRUISE 26

W.C. Fields

OH, HELLO!

Like so many revolutions, movements, and hare-brained ideas, this little cookery book was born in a pub.

The pub is this book's touchstone, and I've listed an excellent choice of drink to go with each recipe. Even though I'm still cooking from this book, opening its pages feels like the past – my past with cooking school and food adventures abroad and the things I've learned (and unlearned) in Red Lions across the country. It's a cookbook as personal biography, and it's a nostalgic feeling as I turn its pages ... Look, I'm obviously not getting weepy over memories of a tuna pasta crispy bake (p 10); that's just the onions I'm cutting up for lunch.

Male bonding rules had my pub mates gently ribbing me for learning to cook and taking some classes. I took the teasing all right, I guess, even if it was kind of confusing now that I think about it. Did they think they were winning by capping their skills at microwaving old toast while I got stuck in with some fiery venison vindaloo?

'Blimey, Andy, why don't you do us up a cookbook, then? Har har.'

They may have put me up to it, but that didn't mean they believed I could do it. The confidence of my mates in me extended to a belief that I could manage an eighth pint of cider, but publishing a lively instructional manual that'll enrich the lives of my countryfolk was quite another matter. 'Yeah, Andy writing a book?! HAR HAR' and 'I won't hold me breath, then' was about the sum of it. Well, gents, I've brought this little baby into the Farmhouse Pub and am now watching you read this introduction. Yes, I will take a congratulatory pint from all of you.

Most of my pub-frequenting friends have their tales of unfortunate cooking incidents. Back from the pub and rip-roaringly hungry, their culinary dreams were dashed by meals that turned out more cordon noir than cordon bleu - never mind the sharp knives, kitchen fires and falling asleep. Yikes! The recipes here are easy enough for you to manage but not intended for lovely readers who are drunk, but rather for those who are drunks. There is a difference.

I've woken up in the morning to find all the rings of my oven on and blazing, and while that makes for a funny little story now, it wasn't so much then. I don't want to be a killjoy, but bodily danger and reducing your flat to a burning ember don't make these recipes taste any better. The obvious answer is to get a takeaway.

Still this isn't always possible, and sometimes we get a bit fed up with that option. Use this book to prepare a meal before you go out, or hand it to a loved one willing to finish things off upon your return – not your mate who you've just been out with. That book is *Cooking with Other Drunks*, which isn't my expertise.

You'll be glad to know that all my ingredients are responsibly sourced (it's my responsibility to source them from the Sainsbury's or Tesco down the way), and I haven't worried about portion sizes; the dishes should feed at least two, but you're probably going to eat the lot anyway. Also, counting calories after that barrel of beer you guzzled doesn't make a lot of sense.

Please view this book in the relaxed, happy spirit that I've written it in. If you can't find an ingredient or two, it probably won't make much difference. I have got a lot out of my journey into food, and if you can break off a piece of that (that's a food metaphor), it makes me glad to share.

With the air of an experienced surgeon, I brought my hands up in front of me, elbows bent with forearms at a ninety-degree angle, and I pulled the latex gloves more firmly onto my hands.

'Precision cooking, my darling. Gloves required.'

I can't remember what my wife thought of that, but the gloves are a necessity. You really, really don't want to be touching any part of your body when you've been messing with red hot chillies. Let's not go down the road of even imagining the possibilities [shiver]. We're eating.

CHILLY WILLY

Fry the chorizo in a sauté pan, constantly turning it until it browns on both sides, then remove it from the pan and put it to one side.

With the oil from the chorizo still in the pan, add the onion. Fry for a couple of minutes and then add the mince. Continue frying until the mince starts to brown while adding the garlic and mushrooms.

Now add the red pepper, tomatoes, kidney beans and chillies.

Add the stock to the pan with the other ingredients. Bring it all to the boil, then cover and turn it down to simmer for 30 minutes.

Switch off the stove and go to the pub for a couple while it marinates.

Upon your return, ask someone helpful to switch it back on and put on some rice.

Cook for a further 20 minutes and serve with Parmesan.

DIFFICULTY LEVEL	***
PREFERRED BEER	Stella
COOKING TIME	90 mins

- **90 g** – spicy Spanish chorizo, sliced
- **1** – large red onion, finely chopped
- **500 g** – extra-lean beef mince
- **2** – garlic cloves, grated
- **200 g** – mushrooms, chopped
- **1** – red pepper, chopped
- **400 g** – tin of chopped tomatoes
- **400 g** – tin of red kidney beans in chilli sauce
- **5** – red bird's eye chillies, finely chopped
- **500 ml** – beef stock
- **2 tsp** – hot chilli powder
- **2 tsp** – smoked paprika
- **1 tsp** – ground coriander
- **1 tbsp** – tomato purée
- – Parmesan cheese, grated

As trusty as these recipes are, a takeaway makes more sense after a long night at the pub.

DIFFICULTY LEVEL	***
PREFERRED CIDER	Strongbow
COOKING TIME	60 mins

On my birthday, I splurged £100 and asked my local Chinese (actually run by local Chinese, if you catch my meaning) to bring a load of the good stuff round the house for everyone. This was a great idea in theory, but you know how when the energy in the pub is up and you're still pretty thirsty, and leaving just seems like a bad idea?

So we called to delay the delivery. Then we called again. My friend Karen raised an eyebrow.

Then we called again.

Then we ... you get the idea. Karen, bless her, was getting the hump at all the delays, so she went back to my house to take the delivery. When she answered the door, the strains of 'Happy Birthday' hit her in heavily accented English from a trio of deliverymen. This was hilARIOUS to us, but Karen didn't think it was so funny in the telling. Poor Karen.

KUNG POO CHICKEN

2 – chicken breasts, diced

1 tbsp – sesame oil

4 – spring onions, thinly sliced lengthways

2 – garlic cloves, grated

1 – red pepper, thinly sliced

3 – red bird's eye chillies, finely chopped

– cashew nuts (responsibly sourced from the pub)

Sauce

1 tbsp – cornflour

2 tbsp – Shaoxing rice wine

2 tbsp – soy sauce

1 tbsp – hoisin sauce

2 tbsp – sugar

1 tsp – fresh ginger, grated

300 ml – water

Mix the sauce ingredients in a bowl and set aside.

Lightly fry the chicken in a wok or sauté pan with the sesame oil. Just before it starts to brown, add the spring onions and garlic.

Continue frying for a few minutes until the chicken starts to brown, but don't let the garlic burn.

Add the red pepper, chillies and sauce along with a handful of cashews.

Cover and simmer for 20 minutes.

Serve on a bed of rice with a couple of pancake rolls.

A nice change from curry, this.

'Sausages amuse me'

I'll just come out and say it: sausages amuse me. So when our local farm shop advertised a sausage-making course, my mate Sid and I were all over it: a morning spent learning how to make the things and tie them up like butchers do!

Basking in the glow of our new-found skills, not to mention an appreciation for all the labour that goes into just one aspect of our breakfast that we wolf down, those sly dogs at the farm marched us over to the shop for the hard sell: a sausage machine.

Well, the elaborate ploy might have worked, but when I gave the shiny new toy some careful consideration, it worked out that using it to make my own rolled packets of meaty goodness for 37 years of very regular sausage consumption would see me break even.

We decided to give it a miss. Best bet is your local butcher.

DIFFICULTY LEVEL	**
PREFERRED BEER	Singha
COOKING TIME	40 mins

THAI LADYBOY SURPRISE

In a wok or sauté pan, add the sausages to the sesame oil and gently fry them till they're golden brown. After removing them from the pan, slice each one lengthways into two.

Add the spring onions to the hot wok and fry them for 2 minutes. Add the curry paste, coconut milk, stock, garlic and chillies and finally your sausage.

Fry it all for 3 minutes, stirring continually, then add the noodles.

Cook everything for a further 2-3 minutes, then serve with soy sauce to taste.

6 – chilli sausages

2 tsp – toasted sesame oil

4 – spring onions, sliced lengthways

2 tbsp – red Thai curry paste

250 ml – coconut milk

300 ml – vegetable stock

2 – garlic cloves, grated

3 – red bird's eye chillies, finely chopped

150 g – straight-to-wok noodles

– soy sauce

PAELLA VALENCIANA

We found ourselves in a charming paella restaurant in the birthplace of paella, Valencia, Spain. But I wasn't thinking about any of that. I was tucking into a few glasses of wine to calm my nerves before popping the question. I was so nervous, and I kept looking around shiftily, waiting for the restaurant to clear a bit. My lovely girlfriend Suzanne was momentarily distracted – Heck, now was the time! With all my jitters, going down on one knee wasn't the smoothest operation. Should I have practised first?! Argh, too late! She's turning around … !

A combination of timing, the position of the table, and my knee-bending meant that she looked back to where I was and thought,

'God, he's fallen off his chair!'

Couldn't tell you why that was her first thought, but anyway, she said yes.

2 tbsp	olive oil
1	chicken breast, cubed
80 g	spicy Spanish chorizo, sliced
1	frozen cod fillet
100 g	mushrooms, chopped
1	large red onion, finely chopped
20 g	butter
120 g	long-grain rice
500 ml	chicken stock
200 g	king prawns, cooked
1	red pepper, chopped
1 tsp	ground coriander
2 tsp	smoked paprika
1 tsp	turmeric
3	red bird's eye chillies, finely chopped
2 tsp	fresh basil, chopped
2	garlic cloves, grated

DIFFICULTY LEVEL	✳✳✳
PREFERRED BEER	San Miguel
COOKING TIME	80 mins

In a sauté pan, use half the oil to fry the chicken breast until it's nearly brown. Add the chorizo and fry both sides of it until they just start to brown. Remove everything from the pan and set it to one side.

Place the frozen fish in a bowl, cover it with cling film and pierce. Put the bowl in the microwave for 2-3 minutes on high and then drain the fish.

Break the fish into smaller pieces and add it to the chicken and chorizo.

Gently heat the remaining oil in the sauté pan. When it's hot, add the mushrooms and onion and fry them for a few minutes until soft, then move them to one side of the pan.

In butter, gently fry the uncooked rice for 2 minutes without browning, then add the stock.

Stir in the chicken, prawns and fish. Add the pepper, spices, chillies, basil and garlic.

Cover and simmer for 20 minutes.

Remove the cover for the final 10 minutes until most of the liquid is gone.

Food as memory

The world is a small place, isn't it? My journey with cooking has brought the world home to me, in a way.

Our lovely friend Doe isn't with us anymore, but I talked to her about this book. Her history in the Caribbean adds just the sort of richness I wanted to build these recipes on.

We all really miss Doe, and my version of jerk chicken will never match hers. I can picture her smiling, putting her hand on my arm and chuckling, 'It's getting there, Andy'.

JAMAICAN JERK

12 – chicken drumsticks

2 – limes, cut into wedges

Marinade

2 – Scotch bonnet chilli peppers, deseeded

3 – garlic cloves

1 tbsp – thyme, leaves only

1 tbsp – fresh ginger

2 tbsp – dark soy sauce

2 tbsp – brown sugar

2 tsp – Worcester sauce

1 tbsp – olive oil

2 tsp – ground allspice

1 tsp – black pepper

1 tbsp – lime juice

– bunch of spring onions, topped and tailed

Set aside the chicken drumsticks and lime wedges.

Rough chop the onions and deseed the peppers. Make sure you wear gloves when handling Scotch bonnets!

Place the remainder of the ingredients in a blender for the marinade. Blast until a smooth paste is achieved.

Put the drumsticks on a baking tray and coat them with the paste. Refrigerate them for a minimum of 2 hours, but preferably overnight.

Cook the drumsticks in a preheated oven at 200ºC / fan 180ºC / gas mark 6 for 30 minutes, and then transfer them to a barbecue or place them under a grill until the chicken is brown and cooked.

Serve with lime wedges.

DIFFICULTY LEVEL	**
PREFERRED DRINK	rum & Coke
COOKING TIME	60 mins

SEAMAN'S FISHY PIE

In a large saucepan start boiling the potatoes.

In a sauté pan, add the milk and fish and poach for 5-6 minutes until the skin is removable.

Strain the used milk and add with half the butter to a saucepan, and bring it to the boil. Reduce the heat and stir in half of the flour and all of the wine and parsley.

Simmer for 3-4 minutes until a creamy sauce is achieved, adding flour if necessary.

Place the fish in an ovenproof dish, then add the prawns, mushrooms and sweetcorn. Pour the sauce over it all, stirring well.

Once they're soft, mash the potatoes with the rest of the butter and spread them over the fish with a fork.

Grate the cheese over the top and sprinkle with pepper.

Bake at 200ºC / fan 180ºC / gas mark 6 for 30 minutes until the top has browned.

DIFFICULTY LEVEL	***
PREFERRED WINE	white
COOKING TIME	90 mins

1 kg	potatoes, peeled and halved
450 ml	semi-skimmed milk
250 g	boneless smoked haddock fillets
130 g	boneless salmon fillets
50 g	butter
50 g	plain white flour
1 tbsp	fresh parsley, chopped
200 g	king prawns, cooked
50 g	button mushrooms
50 g	frozen sweetcorn
100 g	mature cheddar, grated
	half a glass of white wine
	black pepper

Catch of the Day

When you're in the pub with the fireplace roaring and some lovely grub in front of you, the idea of being cold, tired and beerless out on the water in an open boat doesn't appeal. Still, my mate Dave talked me into going sea fishing (probably after the third or fourth pint). Protests that I didn't have the gear fell short because Dave had everything; we packed it all in my car and headed off to Shoreham.

As we parked, it became clear that the car park and the jetty we wanted to fish from were a fair distance apart. We'd come that far, of course, so we grabbed our gear and marched for a good ten minutes across a pebbly beach.

It looked like luck wasn't on our side; all we caught were a few tiddlers.

Well, that was fun! But we obviously weren't near a pub, so we packed everything up for the trek back to the car.

I walked to the boot and reached in my pocket. As the realisation that my keys were gone took shape, my heart sank lower than my lure ever did. I looked back on the wide grey expanse of pebbles and sticks and debris ... and I despaired. There was no way I would find a small silver-grey object in all that. (Why, oh why did I ever leave the ruddy pub?)

Still, needs must, so without any real evidence of our path, we tried to retrace our steps.

By some miracle, we found the keys.

To all the friends and family and pubgoers asking if I'd had any luck fishing, well, I certainly did. I should've snapped one of those big-catch photos fishermen always take, but just with me dangling my keys and smiling.

Catch of the Day!

CARNAGE CASSEROLE

Mally and the deer

My accountant Mally was driving innocently along, and he had a very unfortunate collision with a deer, antlers and all. Apparently there's some rule against taking a carcass home unless someone else hit it? Besides, Mally would say the deer hit him, not the other way around. The deer may have had another read on it, but you know accountants, always seeing different things in the numbers. Still, both Mally and the deer would agree that it was, you know ... carnage.

Sorry.

1 – large rabbit, portioned into 6 pieces (or road kill if still warm)

1 tbsp – olive oil

2 – large yellow onions, chopped

500 ml – chicken stock

150 ml – red wine

3 – carrots, chopped fairly large

1 – red pepper, chopped fairly large

3 – potatoes, chopped fairly large

4 – mushrooms, whole

1 – bay leaf

1 tbsp – plain flour

2 – garlic cloves, grated

– salt and black pepper

You need to be organised with this one by getting it ready before you go out. Top tip: set the oven timer to switch off, as you're bound to be late getting back.

Begin by gently frying the rabbit in a frying pan until it starts to brown.

Add the onions and continue frying for a few minutes.

Place it all in a casserole dish and cover it with the stock and wine.

Add the carrots, pepper, potatoes and mushrooms along with the rest of the ingredients. Add salt and pepper to taste.

Cook for 2½ hours at 170ºC / fan 150ºC / gas mark 3.

DIFFICULTY LEVEL	**
PREFERRED BEER	Guinness
COOKING TIME	190 mins

Caws pobi, anyone?

Chaps, ladies, don't cheat on this one: placing the toaster on its side and cooking everything in there is a baaaaaaaad idea. Seriously. Besides, we feel like a whole book on drunk cooking is sort of helping you cheat anyway, so let's not push it.

WELSH BEANIE RAREBIT

Mix the mustard and Guinness in a pan until it turns into a runny paste. Add the cheese, butter and Worcester sauce. Heat the mixture until the cheese has melted without boiling. Remove the pan from the heat and mix in the egg.

Open the beans and simmer them in a saucepan on the hob.

Place the bread under the grill and toast it – but only lightly on the cheese side!

Remove the toast and spread the cheese goo over it followed by some pepper.

Place it under the grill until it browns.

Plate the result and pour the beans over it all for a tasty finish.

DIFFICULTY LEVEL	*
PREFERRED BEER	real ale
COOKING TIME	25 mins

- **2 tsp** – English mustard
- **3 tbsp** – Guinness
- **200 g** – medium cheddar, grated or chopped
- **1 tsp** – butter
- **2 tsp** – Worcester sauce
- **1** – large egg, beaten
- **4** – slices of thick granary bread
- – tin of baked beans
- – black pepper

TUNA PASTA CRISPY BAKE

The missing link

Maybe I'm vain or just enjoy the chats and Italian coffee, but I find myself sitting in the chair of my barber Tony on a weekly basis. Tony calls this dish *Cuocere la pasta di tonno,* which we both agree sounds better.

But what's the connection between my fish recipe and a haircut?

Well, um, let me see ... tuna pasta crispy bake ... fish and pasta ... fish on Friday and Italy ... I get my haircut on Fridays from Tony the Italian.

Ha! Got there in the end.

DIFFICULTY LEVEL	**
PREFERRED WINE	Frascati
COOKING TIME	60 mins

Boil the pasta until slightly undercooked. Carefully melt the butter in a saucepan, then mix in the flour. Slowly mix in the milk to create a sauce. Remove from heat and stir in the mustard and garlic. Season with salt and pepper.

Put the tuna, drained pasta, sweetcorn and half the cheese in a shallow ovenproof dish. Pour over the sauce and mix everything well.

After sitting on the crisps, sprinkle them on top followed by the remainder of the cheese.

Cook for 30 minutes at 200ºC / fan 180ºC / gas mark 6 until the top is golden brown.

300 g	fusilli
50 g	butter
50 g	plain flour
600 ml	semi-skimmed milk
2 tsp	English mustard
2	garlic cloves, grated
320 g	tuna chunks
100 g	tinned sweetcorn
200 g	mature cheddar, grated
2	packets of crisps
	salt and black pepper

How the story ends

I was standing in the unfamiliar space of a foreign butcher's shop, in a French town near an airfield where we were camping and taking in an airshow. A group of us used to travel together back in the day when we were still carefree and time-rich, nothing stopping us from crossing borders to barbecue and drink. Sure, it's the same thing we did back home, but with aeroplanes and French stuff. We loved it.

And we love our food, of course. Because all our meals were prepared at the campsite, we were getting a little tired of burgers. But you can do this Bolognese on the barbecue, no problem. Guaranteed easy dinner.

I still remember how good that mince at the butcher's looked: it was glossy with no white bits, and I spied it right away. When I motioned to it using my best French pointy finger, the chap behind the counter gave me a blank stare and said, 'Cheval'.

My heart didn't sink right away because I wasn't immediately sure what he meant. Plus, I had drunk a lot of beers back at camp.

If you're wondering how the story ends, let me just say that it was really, really good-looking mince.

DIFFICULTY LEVEL	**
PREFERRED WINE	Chianti
COOKING TIME	2 hrs

PARISIAN BOLOGNESE

Heat the olive oil in a sauté pan at a medium heat, then add the chopped onion and fry it for 2 minutes.

Add the mince, bacon and mushrooms, stirring continually until the mince starts to brown.

Add the garlic, oregano, and Worcester sauce, and keep stirring for another minute. Stir in the tinned tomatoes, red wine, purée and the stock.

Reduce the heat to a simmer and cover the pan with the lid.

Cook for an hour, stirring occasionally, then add the basil and season to taste. Continue cooking with the pan uncovered for a further 30 minutes.

Meanwhile, add your spaghetti to a pan of boiling water until it is soft. Drain and rinse.

Serve the Bolognese on a bed of spaghetti sprinkled with Parmesan cheese.

1 tbsp	olive oil
1	large red onion, finely chopped
500 g	extra-lean beef mince (cheval optional)
5	rashers of smoked bacon, finely sliced
200 g	mushrooms, chopped
2	garlic cloves, grated
1 tsp	dried oregano
2 tsp	Worcester sauce
400 g	tin of chopped tomatoes
150 ml	red wine
1 tbsp	tomato purée
350 ml	beef stock
300 g	spaghetti, broken up
	Parmesan cheese, grated
	handful of fresh basil, chopped
	salt and black pepper

Six alarms but no fire

DIFFICULTY LEVEL	***
PREFERRED BEER	Peroni
COOKING TIME	65 mins

REVENGE PRAWN

This dish is really *king prawn, chicken and chorizo linguine,* but it so needed this title.

Place the linguine in a pan and boil it for 10–15 minutes until it is soft.

In a sauté pan, fry the chicken in olive oil until cooked through.

Move the chicken to the outside of the pan and lightly cook the chorizo on both sides until it starts to brown. Stir the chicken into it and again move everything to the sides of the pan.

Add another drop of olive oil, then add the plum tomatoes. Season them with salt and pepper, and cook them till they are just soft.

Add the prawns, garlic, chilli, onions, red pepper and spices, and cook for 2 minutes.

Stir in the contents of the tomato tin, then drain and rinse the linguine and add it along with the basil.

Cook on high for a further 5 minutes, stirring constantly.

Serve with Parmesan cheese and pepper.

Every week we eat this. Every week. When we're out for dinner I find it hard to order the fish because I might miss out on some properly cooked meat, but this dish has it all, including the chorizo and chilli powder that keep popping up in these pages.

Tesco does a nice, spicy version of the chorizo, and I'm throwing bird's eye chillies in all kinds of things these days. We're liking things hotter and hotter, but Suzanne has had so much chilli in everything that I'm worried she's not feeling it anymore.

I'm now at the point of adding six bird's eyes to these dishes, and I've literally got beads of sweat rolling down my face, it's mental, and Suzanne will tuck in and go 'Oh, this is nice'.

200 g	Italian linguine, broken up
1	chicken breast, cubed
1 tbsp	olive oil
80 g	spicy chorizo, sliced
200 g	baby plum tomatoes, halved
160 g	king prawns, cooked
2	garlic cloves, grated
2	red bird's eye chillies, finely chopped
5	spring onions, sliced lengthways
1	Romano red pepper, sliced into strips
1 tsp	hot chilli powder
½ tsp	turmeric
1 tsp	smoked paprika
200 g	tin of chopped tomatoes
	handful of fresh basil, chopped
	Parmesan cheese, grated
	salt and black pepper

The physics of late-night grub

I was first in the queue at the kebab shop. We were down the pub for a few pints, Martin and I, and it's Newtonian physics or something that says drunk particles will end up near greasy late-night food or else you risk creating a singularity.

I didn't have time to ponder the physics, though, because my kebab was ready, so I thanked the gent behind the counter and went outside to sort out my hunger. I figured Martin would be a while as the shopkeeper puts extra everything on Martin's doner and then puts more meat on it.

That sounds like I'm making a joke, but it's accurate for Martin. The lad could eat. When we were out with my sister in Dublin for a filling Chinese dinner, Martin grabbed a kebab on our way home.

Anyway, I'm outside, and out comes Martin in a pose that in any other circumstance would cause no suspicion: he was standing next to a kebab shop window holding a medium kebab.

Only I knew something was very wrong. A black hole orbited where Martin's stomach should have been, and it would not be filled with this dwarf star of a doner.

He looked at me with the composure of a scientist who knew the results of the experiment before it started: 'Mate, this is just my interim kebab while they make me the big one'.

Science was saved.

DIFFICULTY LEVEL	**
PREFERRED BEER	Amstel
COOKING TIME	65 mins

FAB KEBAB

Marinade

200 g	Greek yogurt
1 tbsp	olive oil
2	garlic cloves, grated
2	red bird's eye chillies, finely chopped
½ tsp	dried cumin
1 tsp	dried oregano
½ tsp	ground cinnamon
2 tsp	unsmoked paprika
1 tsp	black pepper
½ tsp	turmeric
2 tbsp	lemon juice

Kebab

3	chicken breasts, cut into large cubes
1	red pepper, chopped into large pieces
1	green pepper, chopped into large pieces
2	large red onions, chopped into large pieces
4	pitta breads
6	metal kebab skewers
	lettuce, shredded
	jalapeño peppers
	hot chilli sauce

In a bowl combine the yogurt, olive oil, garlic and chillies and stir till they are well mixed together.

Add the cumin, oregano, cinnamon, paprika, pepper, turmeric and lemon juice and give it another good stir.

Thread your skewers alternating between chicken, pepper and onion.

Lay your kebabs in a shallow dish and cover them completely on both sides with the marinade.

Cover the dish and place it in the fridge for a minimum of 2 hours but preferably overnight.

Cook the skewers on a BBQ or under a grill on medium heat for 20-25 minutes till the chicken appears brown and cooked through.

Serve with the pitta bread, lettuce, jalapeños and chilli sauce.

Sour grapes

My growing love of cooking saw me exploring and talking about the ingredients themselves. I started to care more about where my food came from, even if I was careful not to look too earnest about it at the pub. Still, I was excited about the chilli plant I spent half a year of my life growing to support this recipe.

Did I say 'spent half a year'? I meant 'practically wasted six months'. The amount of effort I put into shepherding a full dozen chilli plants in my garden from seedling to a couple of somewhat workable specimens ... well, I was hotter than a Red Amazon pepper when I went round to my mate Ray's gaff to see his magnificent flowering plant chock-a-block with juicy chillies that he got from Waitrose for three quid.

I looked at Ray and thought bitterly, 'You've got to be kidding me'. So there were some sour grapes (even *they* were healthier than my chillies), and it occurred to me in that exasperating moment that Ray wasn't much of a cook, so why did he even possess such a thing? But that's the kind of private thought that you don't share unless you're publishing a book.

LAMB ROGAN GOSH!

DIFFICULTY LEVEL	★★★
PREFERRED BEER	Cobra
COOKING TIME	75 mins

In a sauté pan, gently fry the lamb in half the vegetable oil to seal it. Remove the lamb from the pan and set it to one side.

With the remaining oil, gently fry the onion until it's soft and then add the garlic.

Add the lamb, chillies, ginger, curry powder and turmeric, and fry it all up till you can smell the spices but before it starts to burn (1 or 2 minutes).

Add the tomatoes, water and purée, then cover and gently simmer for 30 minutes.

Add the yogurt and coriander, and continue cooking uncovered for 10 minutes.

Serve with basmati rice and a garlic nan.

400 g	lamb leg or shoulder, cubed
2 tbsp	vegetable oil
1	large yellow onion, finely chopped
3	garlic cloves, grated
3	red bird's eye chillies, finely chopped
2 tsp	fresh ginger, grated
1 tbsp	madras curry powder
1 tsp	turmeric
200 g	tin of chopped tomatoes
300 ml	water
2 tbsp	tomato purée
100 g	Greek yogurt
	handful of fresh coriander, chopped

Six bells of $%&@!

As kids in England, we never got a crack at a piñata. The closest we came was Pin the tail on the donkey. I prefer the Mexicans' more full-on approach. It's a bit like their food: no subtle flavours going on there – just bang there you go.

I am not an angry man, but knocking six bells of $%&@! out of something with sticks looks like a lot of fun.

FAJITAS

Place the chicken strips in a bowl and add the mixed marinade ingredients. Place the bowl in the fridge for a couple of hours.

Heat the oil in a hot wok, and fry the chicken until it's cooked and slightly brown on both sides. Remove the chicken from the wok and place it to one side.

Fry the onion and red pepper until they're soft, then add the garlic, chillies and chicken. Continue frying for another 3 minutes, stirring constantly.

Heat the wraps in the microwave for 30 seconds on high.

Serve by spreading the yogurt on the wraps, then adding the mixture. Roll and enjoy.

2 –	chicken breasts, cut into thin strips
1 tbsp –	sunflower oil
1 –	large red onion, sliced top to bottom into thin slices
1 –	red pepper, sliced into thin strips
2 –	garlic cloves, grated
2 –	red bird's eye chillies, finely chopped
8 –	medium tortilla wraps
250 g –	Greek yogurt

Marinade

1 tbsp –	sunflower oil
2 tbsp –	lime juice
2 tsp –	smoked paprika
2 tsp –	ground coriander
2 tsp –	hot chilli powder
½ tsp –	dried cumin

DIFFICULTY LEVEL	**
PREFERRED BEER	Corona
COOKING TIME	30 mins

Two Sids to every story

I've got two mates called Sid, and they've got a couple of things in common: both of them are electricians, and neither of their real names are Sid.

Sid, who lives in the West Country, came up to do some electrical work for me that would take a few weeks, but he went back home midway through to finish a job. Having arrived at mine in his tatty old Land Rover, he was happy to take my Astravan to make the trek back.

When he returned to mine, the van was hoovered, wiped down, and the interior had even enjoyed a dose of air freshener. I was happy for him to use the van; it didn't need to come back so clean.

'No need to do all that, mate', I insisted. Sid explained that while he was on the job at a local pig farm, he'd left the boot open, thinking the dangers of failing to secure his vehicle in the West Country were pretty meagre.

Depends on what you mean by danger, I guess. When Sid got back to the van, a full-grown sow had made her way into the back, spread herself around and was refusing to move.

Almost like a very sticky pork fillet.

400g – pork tenderloin

4 tsp – toasted sesame oil

150g – pack of mixed Chinese vegetables for stir-fry

300g – fresh Singapore rice noodles

4 – hot green chillies, finely chopped

Marinade

4 tbsp – clear honey

3 tbsp – hoisin sauce

2 tbsp – soy sauce

2 – garlic cloves, grated

2 tbsp – tomato ketchup

½ tsp – Chinese five-spice

1 tbsp – muscovado sugar

1 tsp – hot chilli powder

DIFFICULTY LEVEL	★★★
PREFERRED CIDER	Bulmers
COOKING TIME	65 mins

VERY STICKY PORK FILLET

Preheat the oven to 210ºC / fan 190ºC / gas mark 5.

In a mixing bowl add all of the marinade ingredients and stir them well.

Place the pork tenderloin in a bowl and coat it with 2 tablespoons of the marinade. Cover it and place in the fridge for at least an hour.

In a large sauté pan heat half the oil till it's hot, then sear the pork on all sides for 3-4 minutes until it just starts to brown.

Transfer the fillet to a baking tin lined with tinfoil. Spoon nearly the rest of the marinade over it but save 2 tablespoons for basting. Cover the fillet with foil and place it in the oven.

After 20 minutes take the tin out and remove the foil. Baste the fillet with the rest of the sauce and return it to the oven uncovered for a further 20 minutes.

Remove the tin from the oven, leave the fillet to rest on a plate, and keep the sauce that is left in the tin as a dressing.

Fry the vegetables in a wok with the remainder of the oil for a couple of minutes and then add the noodles.

Continue to fry it all up for 2-3 minutes and then serve it with the pork and sauce. Garnish with the chillies if you like it hot.

I didn't go all the way to Mauritius to catch crabs. Far from it, actually: I was on my honeymoon.

We loved this dish, so when we got home I made my own version.

MAURITIAN CRAB BOUILLON

Fry the onions in olive oil until they are soft and transparent, then add the garlic and ginger for a further minute.

Stir in the tomatoes, stock, chillies, thyme and parsley. Simmer everything for 5 minutes until the sauce is well mixed.

Add the crab and simmer for 45 minutes. The crab should turn red.

Add salt and pepper to taste and serve with crusty bread.

1	large red onion, chopped
1 tbsp	olive oil
3	garlic cloves, chopped
1 tsp	fresh ginger, grated
400 g	tin of chopped tomatoes
300 ml	chicken stock
2	green chillies, chopped
2	red chillies, chopped
1 tbsp	thyme leaves
1 tbsp	fresh parsley, chopped
500 g	cleaned crab, cut into large pieces
	salt and black pepper

DIFFICULTY LEVEL	★★★
PREFERRED BEER	Phoenix
COOKING TIME	75 mins

Russ vs Nikos

Some of my mates caught the cooking bug as well, and Russ was one of them, but when someone new moved into his flat, it was a bit disappointing for Russ that he still ended up doing all the cooking. Turns out that Nikos was a nice bloke and a good flatmate, but useless in the kitchen.

Down at the pub, the barman asked Russ if Nikos had prepared anything nice since moving in. 'You're joking,' scoffed Russ. 'He can't cook'.

The barman got a look, and then, with the wisdom of someone who's heard it all, relaxed his puzzled face and smiled. 'Ah, that's strange', he offered cheerfully. 'Nikos is a fully trained chef'.

For a little while after, Russ never seemed to have enough ingredients to make a meal for two.

GREEK ISLAND MOUSSAKA

DIFFICULTY LEVEL	****	
PREFERRED DRINK	ouzo	
COOKING TIME	80 mins	

- **3** – potatoes, chopped into 4 mm slices
- **2** – aubergines, chopped into 4 mm slices
- **1** – red onion, chopped
- **2** – garlic cloves, grated
- **1 tbsp** – olive oil
- **500 g** – minced lamb
- **200 g** – tin of chopped tomatoes
- **2** – red chillies, chopped
- **1 tsp** – smoked paprika
- **1 tsp** – dried oregano
- **1 tsp** – hot chilli powder
- **1 tbsp** – fresh parsley, chopped
- **2 tbsp** – tomato purée
- – a glass of red wine

Sauce

- **200 g** – Greek yogurt
- **1** – large egg
- **30 g** – Parmesan cheese, grated

On two baking trays lay the sliced potatoes on one and the sliced aubergines on the other.

Bake for 10 minutes at 210ºC / fan 190ºC / gas mark 7, turning over halfway so both sides brown evenly. Set the potatoes and aubergines to one side.

Gently fry the onion and garlic in olive oil, being careful not to burn the garlic.

Add the minced lamb to brown it, then add the tomatoes, chillies, paprika, oregano and chilli powder. Add the wine, parsley, and tomato purée, then gently fry everything for 12 minutes.

Mix the yogurt, egg and Parmesan together to create a smooth sauce.

In a buttered gratin dish arrange a layer of potatoes followed by a layer of aubergines and then a meat layer. Continue with this pattern until the dish is mostly full.

Pour the sauce over your layers and bake for at least 30 minutes at 190ºC / fan 170ºC / gas mark 5 until the top is brown.

MOROCCAN LAMB TAGINE

Whose is better?

Hilary cooked up a top lamb tagine (in a tagine, of course) – it was the first one I ever saw or ate. Sensing my enthusiasm (I said out loud, 'Cor, I want one of those'), she stepped in. Maybe asking for a handmade version was a little much, but Hilary works for an accountant with a kitchen supplier client who had some liquidated stock, including a tagine, so who am I to complain?

And so my experiments began until I arrived at a recipe that was good enough for a cookbook ... for drunks.

When asked by my editor whether my recipe was better than the original, I laughed nervously. Hilary is someone who definitely knows what she's doing in the kitchen, so I really wouldn't like to say ... I have come a long way with this one, though, and my version makes a smashing winter dish; it has a lot in common with a comforting stew .... Look, we are round to Hilary's for dinner a lot ... Okay, my answer is that hers is definitely better than mine. Yep, that's my answer.

DIFFICULTY LEVEL	★★★★
PREFERRED BEER	Budweiser
COOKING TIME	160 mins

If you have an actual tagine, great! (The dish and the meal share the same name.) If not, a casserole dish will be just fine.

In a sauté pan, fry the lamb for a few minutes in half the olive oil to gently seal it, then remove it from the heat and place it to one side, saving the oil and juices in the pan.

Add the onion to the pan with the remainder of the oil and fry it until soft. Add the garlic, ginger, honey, turmeric, cinnamon, cumin and paprika, and fry it all for a further minute, stirring constantly.

Add the stock to the pan with the lamb and tomatoes and bring to the boil for a couple of minutes.

Switch off the stove and allow everything to cool for a couple of minutes, then transfer it to the casserole dish (or tagine).

Put your dish in the oven for 2 hours at 160ºC / fan 140ºC / gas mark 3, then add the apricots and almonds and salt and pepper to taste, then return it to the oven for 30 minutes.

Serve with couscous.

500 g	lamb, diced
1 tbsp	olive oil
1	large red onion, chopped
2	garlic cloves, grated
1 tbsp	fresh ginger, grated
1 tbsp	honey
1 tsp	turmeric
1 tsp	cinnamon
2 tsp	cumin
2 tsp	paprika
500 ml	vegetable stock
4	tomatoes, quartered
100 g	dried apricots
30 g	flaked, toasted almonds
	salt and black pepper

VENISON VINDALOO

DIFFICULTY LEVEL	****
PREFERRED BEER	Tiger
COOKING TIME	110 mins

Make sure the deer is not still running around.

Fry the onion in olive oil until it is soft and transparent. Add the garlic, ginger, chillies and chilli powder, cumin, cinnamon and turmeric, then fry it all gently, stirring constantly until you can just start smelling the spices.

Remove this spice mix from the heat and set it aside in a bowl.

Fry the venison in a little olive oil until it is sealed and just starting to brown. Add your spice mix then pour in the stock, potatoes, sugar and red wine. Add salt and pepper to taste.

Cover and simmer for 90 minutes until the venison is tender.

Serve with basmati rice and a cheeky garlic nan.

That should make your hair curl.

Russ vs Bill

My friend Russ had a nice arrangement with the local Indian restaurant: on Friday nights they delivered his dinner, and if he wasn't home they left it outside the front door. He always squared them up the next day.

No word on whether they thought he was always working late. He wasn't. (I'll let you guess where he really was.) Except one night he'd made it home in time for the delivery but fell asleep and was too dead to the world to hear a doorbell.

His flatmate Bill then got home (again, you'll never guess from where), and a tasty curry just waiting for him on the doorstep was too irresistible.

You think that's cheek? The next morning Bill had a preemptive moan at Russ for making a mess by leaving his curry out the night before. Russ couldn't remember whether he ate the curry or not, so he dutifully cleaned up the mess.

I guess the moral of that story is to stay out later.

1	large red onion, finely chopped
2 tbsp	olive oil
3	garlic cloves, grated
2 tsp	fresh ginger, grated
6	red bird's eye chillies, finely chopped
2 tsp	hot chilli powder
1 tsp	cumin powder
1 tsp	ground cinnamon
2 tsp	ground turmeric
500 g	venison, cubed
200 ml	beef stock
200 g	tin of new potatoes
1 tsp	sugar
	a glass of red wine
	salt and black pepper

Homemade, innit?

I love meatballs now. I was in the habit of buying Loyd Grossman Classic Chilli sauce for them, but I can't use the sauce in a book, innit? So I tried to make a good version myself.

I haven't come across a whole lot of variation in terms of the meatball ingredients. I make breadcrumbs because they're nicer fresh in the same way that the herbs from our garden are. I added chilli, of course. Throwing in the linguine as well turns it into something great.

My mouth is watering now. This turns out as nice as anything I've had anywhere else, and we're out for Italian all the time. We've got a nice Italian restaurant in town. I don't think they're going to read this.

MY LITTLE MEATY BALLS

DIFFICULTY LEVEL	****
PREFERRED WINE	Rosso Conero
COOKING TIME	120 mins

In a large mixing bowl add the breadcrumbs, mince, garlic, chillies, half the Parmesan, paprika, oregano, and Italian herbs.

Add the egg and parsley, and while wearing gloves mix it all by hand until it feels dough-like.

Tear pieces off your mixture and roll them between the palms of your hands until you have a 25 mm ball. Place the balls on a large plate, cover them with cling film and place the plate in the fridge for a couple of hours.

To make the sauce add the oil to a sauté pan and fry the onion for a couple of minutes until it's soft.

Add the passata, sun-dried tomatoes, stock, chilli, sugar, purée and basil. Cover it all and leave it to simmer for 30 minutes. Pour the contents of the pan into a jug and set it aside for later.

In a pan of boiling water add the linguine and cook it till it's soft, then drain it and rinse.

Put a little olive oil in your sauté pan and gently fry your meaty balls, constantly turning them so they are brown on all faces and no raw mince is showing.

Add the sauce and then the linguine, cover and simmer everything for 15 minutes.

Serve with fresh grated Parmesan.

100 g	white bread, blitzed in a blender
500 g	extra-lean beef mince
2	garlic cloves, grated
2	red bird's eye chillies, finely chopped
80 g	Parmesan cheese, grated
1 tsp	smoked paprika
1 tsp	dried oregano
1 tsp	Italian seasoning
2	eggs, beaten
1 tbsp	olive oil
200 g	Italian linguine, broken up
	handful of fresh parsley, chopped

Sauce

1 tbsp	olive oil
1	small red onion, finely chopped
400 g	Italian passata
50 g	sun-dried tomatoes, finely chopped
450 ml	beef stock
2	red bird's eye chillies, finely chopped
½ tbsp	sugar
2 tbsp	tomato purée
	handful of fresh basil, chopped

No tumbleweed but plenty of wind

Faithful to the Old West way of cooking, my mate swears by Wi-Fi.

Gary is majorly into the US barbecue scene. We'll be on our way to buy supplies for one of his truly unmissable outdoor parties when an alert pops up on his phone: the heat inside his shiny imported American barbecue (with pizza attachment) is too low for the short shoulder of pork he's been smoking for seven hours. Energised by the frontier spirit, Gary taps the 'heat' button and a hopper sitting in his garden releases wood pellets onto a conveyer belt, which adds them to the fire. The setup adjusts the heat with admirable precision.

When I asked Gary's permission to use his recipe for these beans, however, things got a lot less precise. He was excited and agreed right away, but there was a crucial piece missing: most of the recipe. As I tried to write it down, he was all 'Squirt in some of this' and 'Squeeze in some of that' and 'I dunno, I just cook it, don't I?' Maybe the recipe is on your phone, Gary.

200 g	– slow-cooked pulled pork shoulder
3	– cans of Heinz baked beans (415 g), drained
1	– red pepper, diced
1	– large red onion, diced
2 tbsp	– soft brown sugar
2 tbsp	– yellow mustard
1 tbsp	– Worcester sauce
3 tbsp	– barbecue sauce
1 tbsp	– Frank's RedHot sauce
1 tsp	– steak dry rub
2 tsp	– hickory liquid smoke

GARY'S TEXAS BBQ BEANS

Preheat the oven to 140ºC / fan 120ºC / gas mark 1.

Gary buys a shoulder of pork and smokes it, but we mere mortals without smokers can buy slow-cooked pork shoulder in barbecue sauce from all the supermarkets. It generally takes about 20 minutes in the oven. Then just pull it apart with two forks.

Add the pork, beans, pepper, onion, sugar, mustard and the three sauces to a casserole dish. Add the dry rub and liquid smoke for that Texas-style flavour, then put the lid on the dish.

Bake for 3 hours.

DIFFICULTY LEVEL	**
PREFERRED BEER	Colt 45
COOKING TIME	3 h 45 mins

SHEPHERD'S PYE

DIFFICULTY LEVEL	★★★
PREFERRED WINE	Beaujolais
COOKING TIME	80 mins

Authenticity is overrated

You write a cookbook and then everyone assumes you know what you're doing. And you can assume that if you want: after so many years of doing this, I do my best to make sure we've got something tasty at the end. But this is *Cooking for Drunks* not *Cooking for Cooks,* and so even if shepherd's pie calls for lamb and cottage pie calls for beef (depending on where you're from), I prefer the beef one and I'm spelling it 'Pye' so you can't argue.

1 kg	potatoes, peeled and cut into large pieces
2 tbsp	milk
50 g	butter
125 g	mature cheddar, grated
2 tsp	olive oil
1	medium red onion, finely chopped
500 g	extra-lean beef mince
1	garlic clove, grated
1 tsp	caraway seeds
300 ml	beef stock
2 tsp	Worcester sauce
2 tsp	cornflour
2 tbsp	tomato purée
1 tsp	black pepper
2 tsp	Italian seasoning
	handful of frozen peas

In a large saucepan boil the potatoes, checking them with a fork until they are soft.

Drain the potatoes and add the milk, butter and 50 g of the grated cheese, then mash it all until it's light and fluffy and free from lumps.

In a sauté pan heat the oil then add the onion. Fry it for a few minutes and then add the mince, stirring constantly till the mince browns.

In go the garlic and caraway seeds while you mix and fry everything for a further minute.

Now add the stock, Worcester sauce, cornflour, purée, pepper, seasoning and the frozen peas, and then simmer everything for a few minutes until it thickens and most of the water is gone. Add the result to an ovenproof dish. Spread the mash potato evenly over the mince.

Sprinkle the remainder of the cheese over it and add a twist of black pepper.

Preheat the oven to 200ºC / fan 180ºC / gas mark 6 and bake it for 30 minutes.

SARDINIAN SAUSAGE GNOCCHETTI

En Vogue

Paul moved to Sardinia without a smidgen of Italian to rely on, having bought a house without heat or furniture.

Sid and I flew over there, saw it, and thought, 'Oh, blimey. What have you done?'

To help the effort, we ventured off to the nearest shopping centre for a flat-pack wardrobe, which we brought to the cashier who used her best sign language to point at the box while repeating 'Two! Two!' But we didn't need two; we just needed one.

After much head-shaking and more pointing, it turned out that we *did* need two because the wardrobe came in two parts. We thanked her and got the heck out of there, but just as the slight shame over that episode was fading, a deeper, less escapable embarrassment was building.

Every man and woman within our sight was so put together that we had first assumed they were coming out of church. But it wasn't Sunday. Everywhere we looked gents were in spiffy black trousers and coats that fit, while the women were dressed up for a night out - to our eyes, anyway.

Was this shopping centre connected to a catwalk? If so, our T-shirts and flip-flops were too avant-garde for this lot. We were deeply out of place, and I'll never forget it.

I tried to work some regional magic with this recipe. I don't dress up when I'm cooking gnocchetti, but sometimes as I begin boiling the water, part of me thinks I ought to.

DIFFICULTY LEVEL	**
PREFERRED WINE	Grotta Rossa
COOKING TIME	55 mins

---

300 g – De Cecco Gnocchetti sardi Nº 83 pasta

1 tbsp – olive oil

1 – small yellow onion, chopped

4 – Asda Italian inspired sausages, skins removed

2 – garlic cloves, grated

30 g – shiitake mushrooms

300 g – tin of chopped tomatoes

150 ml – white wine

2 – red bird's eye chillies, finely chopped

– handful of fresh basil, chopped

– Parmesan cheese, grated

– salt and black pepper

Boil a saucepan of water and add the pasta, cooking until al dente. Rinse and set aside for later.

Heat the olive oil in a sauté pan at a medium heat and add the chopped onion and fry it for 2 minutes until it softens.

Add the sausage meat, garlic and mushrooms, stirring continually until the meat starts to brown.

Add the tomatoes, wine, chillies, and basil, keeping a pinch back for garnish. Season with salt and pepper.

Simmer for 20 minutes and then stir in the pasta.

Cook for a further few minutes until the pasta is soft.

Serve with a garnish of basil and Parmesan.

It goes down well

I ordered from Domino's once - just once! - and my punishment was a lifetime of texts shouting about whatever deal they've got on. I'm not falling for it, though; at £20+ it goes against my idea that pizza is what you default to when you've got nothing in the fridge.

I never really got the whole pizza thing anyway. But what I didn't know is that it has a lot to do with quality: when you get a fresh pizza from a proper restaurant or you make your own with good ingredients, it's a whole different story.

Instead of being a Monday night default, pizza is a platform for creativity. Start with a decent dough of your own and you're ready to introduce an explosion of possible flavours.

If there's a thread weaving through my cooking history - besides a drink, obviously - it's heat. I look at a dish with chillies, chorizo, jalapeños or pepperoni, and I want it.

It goes down well, my pizza.

DIFFICULTY LEVEL	✱✱✱
PREFERRED BEER	Budweiser
COOKING TIME	50 mins

PIZZA AMERICANA

The dough

160 ml	warm water
3.5 g	yeast
½ tsp	sugar
2 tsp	olive oil
270 g	'00' grade plain flour
½ tsp	salt

The topping

200 ml	Italian passata
2 x 150 g	balls of mozzarella, sliced
120 g	pepperoni, sliced
4 tbsp	Parmesan cheese, grated
6	jalapeño peppers, sliced
4	red bird's eye chillies, finely chopped
½ tsp	dried oregano
	handful of fresh basil, chopped

The ingredients should make two pizzas as one is never enough.

In a jug, mix the warm water with the yeast, sugar and olive oil and allow it to stand for 5 minutes.

Mix the flour and salt together thoroughly in a bowl. Make a hole in the middle of the flour and slowly pour the water in, gradually mixing the two with clean hands.

Sprinkle some flour on a chopping board and knead the dough for 5 minutes until an elastic consistency is achieved.

Leave the dough in a warm place to rise for an hour.

Divide the dough into two and roll it into a large pancake shape about 3 mm thick. This is your base.

Preheat the oven to 240ºC / fan 220ºC / gas mark 9.

Apply olive oil to some kitchen roll and wipe a baking tray to stop the base sticking to it. Place the pizza base on it, ready for your toppings.

Spoon on the passata and spread it over the base. Add the other ingredients, placing them evenly.

Bake for 15-20 minutes until the dough is brown and the cheese is bubbling.

Inauthentically British

DIFFICULTY LEVEL	****
PREFERRED BEER	Tsingtao
COOKING TIME	75 mins

Suzanne and I go away with Sid and Trea once a year, often on a cruise, and when we have a day between islands or cities, we take advantage of what the ship has to offer, including cooking classes led by instructors who hail from the same places their dishes are from.

The chap leading our Thai class turned out to be Welsh of all things, but we were on holiday and rolling with the punches, and the dish turned out great. In fact, we ate it there on the spot.

After class as my wife saw us walk up empty-handed, she wondered where her portion was.

Now, if I recall my explanation at the time, it was either that there wasn't much left or we weren't allowed to take food out of the kitchen *but more importantly can you believe the chef was Welsh?*

Anyway! No time to figure it all out, darling! I need a break from cooking and it's time for dinner. Let's make our way to the restaurant. I could really go for some Thai...

CHICKEN PAD THAI EN CRUISE

Mix the sauce ingredients in a small saucepan and bring to the boil, then simmer for 5 minutes. Set aside.

In a small frying pan, toast the peanuts until golden brown, then chop them finely for the garnish.

In a wok or sauté pan, heat the oil until it's hot, then add the chicken and keep turning it until it's cooked through.

Add the garlic, spring onions, ginger, pepper and chillies, cooking everything for a further minute.

Move the mixture to one side of the pan, then add the egg, stirring as it scrambles. Mix the pan's contents all together.

In go the prawns, bean sprouts, coriander, cashews and the noodles. Pour over the sauce, turning constantly for about 3 minutes.

Serve with a garnish of fresh coriander, chopped peanuts and a lime wedge.

Sauce

1 tbsp	Shaoxing rice wine
2 tbsp	fish sauce
2 tbsp	tamarind paste
2 tbsp	palm sugar (or brown)
1 tbsp	lime juice

	handful of peanuts
1 tbsp	toasted sesame oil
1	large chicken breast, cut into strips
2	garlic cloves, grated
1	bunch of spring onions, sliced lengthways
1 tsp	fresh ginger, grated
1	Romano red pepper, sliced into strips
2	red bird's eye chillies, finely chopped
2	eggs, beaten
180 g	king prawns, cooked
100 g	bean sprouts
	handful of fresh coriander, chopped
	handful of cashew nuts
150 g	straight-to-wok ribbon rice noodles
1	lime, cut into wedges

NOTES

NOTES

I DISTRUST CAMELS, AND
ANYONE ELSE WHO CAN GO
A WEEK WITHOUT A DRINK.

Joe E. Lewis

NOTES

NOTES

A RECIPE HAS NO SOUL.
YOU, AS THE COOK, MUST
BRING SOUL TO THE RECIPE.

Thomas Keller

NOTES

Andy Sausage lives in a quiet village
in West Sussex with his wife, Suzanne.
He remains an avid cook but his
pub attendance has become
a little less frequent.

I tip my pint gratefully to Terese,
Sid and Ian for their input, and to my
wife, Suzanne, for eating my recipes
on a regular basis.

Lightning Source UK Ltd.
Milton Keynes UK
UKHW051013081019
351188UK00005B/19/P